Observing the Moon

Observing the Moon

Sneha Madhavan-Reese

Hagios Press

A CIP catalogue record for this book is available from Library and Archives Canada.

ISBN: 978-1-926710-36-5

Edited by Harold Rhenisch
Designed and typeset by Donald Ward
Cover Art and Design by Tania Wolk, Go Giraffe Go Inc.
Set in Minioon Pro and Trajan Pro
Printed and bound in Canada at Houghton Boston Printers and Lithographers, Saskatoon.

The publishers gratefully acknowledge the assistance of the Saskatchewan Arts Board, The Canada Council for the Arts, and Creative Saskatchewan in the production of this book.

HAGIOS PRESS
Box 33024 Cathedral PO
Regina SK S4T 7X2
hagiospress@accesscomm.ca
www.hagiospress.com

for John

Take the time to write. You can do your life's work in half an hour a day.

— *Robert Hass*

Contents

Child's Play

Beloved

Daughterhood

Changing Light

Child's Play

Travelling in South India

Palm trees flash past barred windows, and words
waft over the train's noisy pulse. Something is
different — conjugations of verbs, endings of nouns — but I still
understand these pieces of stories on the train
heading east from Vasco da Gama Station.

Vasco himself came
to this place, for spices
and jewels,

and found language
of every hue
and heat. How

did these sound to his
Portuguese ear,
the Malayalam,

Kannada, and Konkani
of the Indian coast?
In three expeditions

to this foreign land,
which of these did he
come to understand?

I understand every language in this part of the world
but one. Telugu speakers switch to Hindi, I revert
to English, and somehow — *Aek masala dosa? No, doh*
masala dosa — I manage to buy my lunch. But in Kerala,
people see only my foreignness, speak only English
in reply to my fluent Malayalam.

Melodious Malayalam
streams with the sun
into the sanctuary of

St. Francis Church
in Kochi. Outside,
two young girls

with hair in braids
drag the heavy gate open
and shut for fun. Inside,

da Gama's first grave, before
his remains were exhumed
and returned to Lisbon.

On the train in India, trees flash past.
Where will my bones belong?
I hear new rhythms: a boy's endless questions
and his mother's explanations. I listen
to these stories in a language I don't know
filled with words I still understand.

Playing Shakespeare

Thin, silky tape between his fingers, my father
on Sunday mornings threaded the reel-to-reel
so he and I could listen to *Othello*.
The *n* of *Desdemona* was nasal and hard
in the actors' strange Shakespeare — Malayalam.

Years later, I studied Shakespeare for myself
and had to read aloud to understand.
His English, rendered in my voice, unwound
crinkled stories long since spooled away.
I read of Desdemona's rapture as
Othello spun his tales, and saw again
the workings of that slowly turning tape:

my childish fidgeting and my father's delight,
his hushing me to hear every word.

The Things My Father Taught Me

Stone steps climb
from Woodward Avenue
to the doors of the downtown library,
a place my father took me when I was young.
He took me to restaurants, too, and museums and musicals,
and he taught me math and chemistry so well
it wasn't until my junior year I learned
something in one of those classes
I hadn't known by the time I was eight.

He taught me Malayalam, his native tongue, not just to speak
but to read and write its curvaceous script. I copied rows
of those luxurious letters with innocent precision.

Time passes
at a speed we perceive
based on our singular days.
I remember the years of my childhood clearly.
Dad picked me up from school each afternoon and fed me
cookies and juice. He recited poems he'd memorized
fifty years before.

Now it's the chatter of the TV,
where my father spends his days
watching signals sent from India
via outer space. How small
the world has become. There are fragments
of poems, but no more books,
no trips to take
or lessons to learn.

At the public library in Detroit,
there is an enormous globe; as a child,
I'd hold the rail to watch it slowly spin.
Today, retired to a side room,
the globe sits motionless,
diminished
and unlit.

Devotion

My father broke coconuts in the laundry room
with his hatchet-like Indian knife. In temples,
they throw the coconuts down, shattering their shells,
spilling their milk as an offering, a sweet sacrifice,
for sweetness in a bitter life. But my young life
was already sweet; maybe this is why we took
the milk for ourselves. I stood at the ready
as my father made measured blows — one, two, three —
until the brown shell cracked, just enough
so he could wedge the blade in
and twist. He held the coconut over the sink
while I held out my glass. Together
we caught the cloudy white liquid, which later
we would share, savouring every sip.

Child's Play

Hands on the table, flip them over,
make two fists, take them away,
aki-lola-koowa-muthi-kanni-lola-kil,

less than a game, just a pattern,
even the young ones soon catch on:
aki-lola-koowa-muthi-kanni-lola-kil.

All come running, kids and grandkids;
teenagers still want to play
aki-lola-koowa-muthi-kanni-lola-kil.

Daddy-Papa (that's my father)
knocks out each phrase on our hands,
aki-lola-koowa-muthi-kanni-lola-kil —

hands on the table, flip them over,
make two fists, take them away —
aki-lola-koowa-muthi-kanni-lola-kil!

Certainty

I.

Every Christmas, after the ritual
gift exchange and *appam* breakfast, we sing
"Happy Birthday" to my dad and share
a store-bought cake.

When he began school, his parents chose
what seemed a normal date, since no one recalled
with certainty
the true date he was born.

When I discovered this, I demanded to learn
their excuse for such neglect. My father, chuckling,
smiled and said, "What need
was there to know?

When rice and *paise* both are scarce,
there is no use for such indulgence."

II.

I was born on May twenty-first
nineteen seventy eight
five oh eight, ante meridian
Eastern Standard Time
Detroit, Michigan, United States
GPS coordinates known,
even elevation: sixth floor
of the hospital downtown.

Such precision was needed,
my mother insisted,
to send for my horoscope.
It arrived in our suburban
mailbox by fall, a life
in a Vedic astrologer's scrawl,
gleaned from his charts
and seashells, and from
the place and moment of my birth.

When I Was a Child

The sun was already high in the sky
when I met my grandmother. My father
held me by the hand and told me
to sit on her lap.

Her face was darker
than any I'd seen, her body all
wrinkles and bone. Tropical dust
clung to my skin, to my lips and fingers and legs
in the wearying heat.

You sit on her lap, I told him,
she's your mother.

Home again, news traveled far
before we learned that she had died.
My mother told me to give Dad a hug. I met his eyes
where he stood, just back from work, framed by the doorway
and evening's pale light. I had his features,
his silence. He had my eyes in his face.

Suddenly, I felt a strange
confusion — a fierce shame, and
something like a wish. I could not rise
to go to him, though I wanted to.

The Caw a Crow Made

Porridge drips, legs dangle from a too-big
spoon, a too-big chair. Adult murmurs fade among
the afternoon haze, the shade of coffee growing
green, and palm trees stretching long necks made
for reaching heaven. The call of an unseen crow,
hidden in that vastness. On the veranda, that spoon

in small hands, the cool twinkle of a spoon
that knows its worth. Simmering curries in big
pots over open fires entice even the crows
with their scent of cardamom and cinnamon rising among
the trees. This solid, reliable spoon was made
to taste a sip of these savory treasures growing

hearty and thick with every stir, growing
from the skill of this spoon. But this poem isn't about a spoon.
There is a woven chair and the caw a crow made,
but the crow is nowhere to be seen. The sun, big
and serene. Did you know that crows are among
the most intelligent of all animals? With its beak, a crow

can fashion a hook out of wire. No wonder crows
are found in stories of every culture, to portend growing
malice, trickery, intellect, divinity. And daring — among
all birds, only a crow will look you in the eye. Could a mere spoon
hold any desire for a creature with such big
connotations? What force they must possess, to have made

such legends of themselves. Here I have made
of them a poem, but then this poem is not about a crow.
Eating bland porridge on the porch in a big
chair, and from that idle afternoon comes a dark shadow, growing,
with open wings, black eyes, and claws reaching for a spoon.
As quickly, it fades, until it disappears among

the trees and the screams, the chaos among
the adults running to see. Then laughter at the fright that made
them run, a child's shout at a crow, swooping to steal her spoon.
They drift back inside, amused at the boldness of the crow,
leaving her alone in a world that never stops growing,
her legs dangling, her fist still closed around that spoon too-big.

Growing up, I made my own world; trees and endless afternoons
were my friends. Always among big things, I was timid until
the day I wrested a spoon from claws and looked a crow in the eye.

Coming Back Around

Red, orange, yellow, green,
blue, indigo, violet —
I teach my daughter *Roy G. Biv*
as we crayon rainbows.

My father's on the other side
of the world, reading Malayalam
magazines in his den. He emerges, looks
over our shoulders and shouts, "*Vib G. Yor!*"
his voice like a foghorn
from the ship that brought him here
to land in Detroit, decades ago. I realize,
in this instant,

how past and future form
not merely an arc but a full circle:

he taught me algebra with *x*'s
drawn as two tangent curves
instead of intersecting lines,

I was teased at school
for pronunciations I'd learned
from him, like
Pa-*naa*-ma Ca-*naal*,

and my Canadian daughter
accents the *a* in *adult*, sings *zed*
at the end of the alphabet instead of *zee*, and already
looks at me as though the things I do and say
are just a bit peculiar, if not
completely backward.

A Giant's Life

Born small, she grew fast,
until she towered over everyone.

Every year her leaves turned golden
and fell, covering the ground.

Every spring they sprouted anew,
blocking the sun. *What to do with her?*

her parents wondered,
Where to send her to school?

She could not hear them so far below.
She listened instead to the birds and clouds.

When winters came, she drifted
into an easy sleep, waking just

as slowly in spring and finding the world
more spectacular than before.

Shedding old leaves one fall, she felt buoyant,
as if she could fly, and she found she *could* move,

though slowly compared to her bird friends.
She explored new lands,

travelled east to the ocean,
then west to another shore.

She returned to her homeland,
years later, but it was no longer hers.

Everyone wanted her to change
not only from what she had become

but from what she had always been.
She was a tree, but they wanted to

fashion her into grasses, as they were.
Stretching her many limbs the following spring,

she decided to leave again.
She knew that those who begged

her to stay would barely notice
she was gone. She didn't know

that one day she would learn
the words of the clouds and the birds,

that one day she would whisper with them
as a sister. Such a life she could not imagine,

yet it would one day be hers: a life of air and light
under a sky rich with space and sun.

Next Time

Sometimes I tell my father about a city
he should visit, and — it being far,
his being almost ninety — he says, "Okay,
next time." Meaning, in his next life,
a new set of chances for catching up,
finishing off, and making right.

My mother reads only religious books, but does
not aim for eternity in this life. "I have to
be born so many times," she says. "No need
for me to meditate just now."

My impulse is to find their faults —

my heart is like the bitter gourd
in my parents' garden — though there is nothing
I wouldn't do for them. Each day I try
to live a deliberate life, knowing my chances are many
but numbered, knowing that someday someone will judge me,

and hoping it will not be too harshly.

Blowing Cold

Growing up, I rarely smiled,
never mind if my mother's scoldings
were warranted: *Smile. Smile bigger.*
It was good manners in our world.

I had a cousin who was always smiling — always polite.
Why can't you be more like her?
Showing my mother her new necklace,
she deflected praise as a nice girl should: *Oh, but it isn't real.*
They both agreed that didn't matter
so long as it looked pretty.

Not real *gold* is what she meant,
though it was real enough to
touch and taste and reflect chandelier light.
It would have been courteous to stay

but I strayed outside, where the wind was steady and strong.

Seeking

Today I read the
Tao Te Ching, and what I found
were Beatles' lyrics.

Autumn Interlude

Trees don their orange vests.
Mercury drops.

Crescendo, cymbal crash: children
walk home from school through mud

puddles. We fall, under the influence of
gravity. The year's routine cracks.

The wind across a girl's cheeks:
an ocean's starry handprint.

Don't stay silent; accumulate.
Rain hits the ground, and runs.

Walking Away

When I was a child, my father
always cut my hair shorter
than I liked. I pleaded,
but the silver shears
moved smoothly behind my neck.
I knew better than to squirm.

As a teenager, I left it long.
Everyone praised its shine.
To me, it was heavy and unkempt.
It was years before I trusted anyone
else with scissors.

Then, short styles. I let
hair dressers experiment.
I had layers, lightness, curls
that kissed my shoulders, ticklish tips
brushing my cheeks, wispy
curves around my ears.

Now, leaving you, my hair
has grown long again,
past my shoulders and
down my back. But instead
of cutting it free, I'll pull it
from my face and drive
home alone, my hair
clasped tightly behind me.

Beloved

On Halloween

for Michele (1978-1997)

Memorial Drive, autumn,
and traffic is stopped tonight,
this night when only
a liminal veil separates
the living and the dead.

Long ago, on this night,
the Celts built huge fires
and masked their faces to become
what they were not, to imitate
the spirits, or to deceive them.

Tonight, tiny fires
dot the street like so many
red eyes. Everyone is in costume,
even the policemen, in their uniforms,
and the river, draped in darkness.

I haven't yet learned
that even our bodies are costumes,
flesh and bones that give us form
and make us creatures of anger
and grief. I haven't yet

learned that the red flares
and police blockade
are for you —
or rather, for your body.
That in an instant —

split seconds between cars,
your trying to cross —
you were hit, and, as you
collapsed, hit again.
It was only weeks ago

when I stood back to watch
you talk with my parents.
You spoke, as I could not,
with a smile on your face.
In those few minutes,

I felt closer to you than ever before
or after. That is a day I will
wish I could remember better,

but I did not yet know
to pay attention.

But Not the Car

for Jeremy (1971-2005)

I can't remember the colour of your car.

The instant oatmeal you microwaved for lunch,
the photos of Carol and the kids,
your tie-dyed shirts, a different explosion of colour
for every day of the week,
but not the car.

Today I am looking out to where it might
have been parked next to mine. The clouds recede to reveal
a blinding sun. A mug of tea,
once steaming, grows cold in my hand.
I remember you, here,

but the colour of the car is as elusive
as smoke rising into a clear sky
after a crash.

Message

Your throaty voice on the machine. A caught breath, in that moment you say my name. The heedless rush of desire. Grief's hesitation.

This Summer

Without you, the grass lies unmowed
and has grown past my knees.

I tried to clear dead branches
from trees in the back, but
the scratches on my arms exploded
into itchy, pink bumps.

Seeing flats of annuals
outside the hardware store, I imagine
neat rows of petunias, alternating
purple and white by the side of the house,
or a wild garden in the open sun
of rudbeckia, bee balm, butterfly weed . . .

But it is too late now
for planting. The summer has come,
with its oppressive heat.

Cutting Out Hearts

At the kitchen table,
I'm practicing on scrap before I tackle
the few sheets of red. Their shapes never please me —
too long, too short, too narrow, too wide.
I know you would help me,
if you were here. You would draw and redraw,
measure and assess, pick up
the tiny scissors and give the task
your full attention. You would present me your heart,
fondant cake on a gilt platter, saying,
Is it not perfect?
Is it not just what you need?

Balance

Half empty, half full?
Look closely — there is only
water in the glass.

Cocktail

for Lisa

Like a shot
in an after-dinner drink,
a dose of lithium —
just what the new doctor
ordered to add to
my friend's cocktail.
Prozac, Zoloft, Nardil, Lexapro . . .
I know nothing of
these, but lithium
in its number three spot
burns red-flamed.
In the body its medicine
fast passes for poison.

What choice do we have?
What else can we try? Why is *try*
the best we can do?

Every night,
a glass of water by
her bed, she
carefully lays out
her pastel pills — a rainbow
to embrace
her every morning.

Wong Tai Sin Fortune-Telling and Oblation Arcade

Adjacent to the smoke-filled temple where women burn
incense by the handful, fortune tellers in their offices
market their soothsaying services. Mrs. Joyce Chan,
so the sign says, provides readings in English.

"Wow" — the first word she says, her lensed eyes
wide, both of my hands open in her own. She inspects the palms
and backs. "You have a man's personality, very stubborn,
very strong," and for a long time she speaks on,
though her accent is impenetrable and my mind is

elsewhere. There is pungent smoke all around, the sound
of bells and chanting and people pushing by each other —
a closeness acceptable, even consoling, in only
a place such as this. We are not alone in our longings.
Worshippers press incense into oranges and apples.

Suddenly her voice is clear, as if she has read my mind:
"You are a family woman. You will have a son
and a daughter who love you, no problem."

The Summer that Laurel Worked at Tosci's

Textbooks aside,
we aspiring
bachelors of science
planned every day
around her shifts.
Friends were always
served for free.

Ice cream, on such
deliberate days,
gives the power
to slow time. How else
could I remember
the way we sat
on the steps of the store
in Central Square
catching all the precious
drips, licking our
cones so carefully
that even now
I can feel the lavish
cold lingering
on my tongue?

Beneath the Riverbed

You turned to me with certain eyes,
your arms around my body, your lips
to my cheek.

                    Your touch:
a pearl in a field of flowers,
an untamed diamond firm within the earth.

Parsing Pillow Talk

Over time,

things we know
well become
beautiful.

We end up
kissing, having
been discussing

electromagnetic waves.

Out of the Blue

We glanced out a dormitory window
before we set out for walks along Marlborough Street
to the Public Garden and after that
the long, green open of the Common. The internet
could have told us more — humidity and wind speed —
but the spire of lights on the Old Hancock
shone for our pleasure alone. Storms raged,
then exited as quickly as they came, out over the harbour.
The beacon even told us, who knew
its secrets, when Red Sox games were cancelled.
In those days, the skies were of our dominion:
Steady blue, clear view. Flashing blue, clouds due.
Steady red, rain ahead. Flashing red, snow instead.

Back in the city where we learned love,
we ride the Green Line train with no idea
we'll soon be drenched. At the Public Garden,
we run without words to our favourite sheltered spot.
Tulips gaze, unfazed, at the sky. In this place, even after a decade,
the ordinary enchants: the slant of sun in late afternoon,
dents in wet grass from our daughter's small feet,
the scent of spring rising after rain.

Thirty Below

Below what, a friend from Florida asks. In frigid February,
with snow blackened and hard, comfort comes from the company
of those who ride the bus. With pants tucked into tall boots,
scarves pulled up and fur-lined hoods pulled down — regalia
that reveals only eyes — they understand
possibilities in scaling snowbanks and waiting in sleet.
Among these hearty comrades, inhibitions fall. I read
books of poetry not caring whether my mouth moves at all.

Words for Snow

I show my daughter the best kind
for sledding, snowmen, and snow angels.

A snowplough on every construction truck.
No two are alike. We fold and cut holes.

Heavy clumps of flakes hit then morph.
Teardrops race down the window.

Every day, the neighbour's cat
straightens his frozen, endless bed.

My green scarf's aging gracefully:
my hair speckled with shards of light.

Berea

On your way from one coast to another,
on a whim, escape the Ohio Turnpike
to a long-gone summer: paths I biked
along the Rocky River, Midwest
small-town streets, and the house
where I used to live, its number
painted on a rock. Drink tea
with my white-haired old landlady,
unwrap gifts she keeps handy
for unexpected guests.

Now, beloved,
one more place that once was mine alone
is also yours.

DAUGHTERHOOD

Mothering

A poem contains meaning
only the way a body contains life. . . .
— Heather McHugh

I love the ocean, her curves
and retreats, the way she carries
herself and the bulk of the world,
weightlessly.

I love the ocean and have wondered
what she feels, having so much
alive inside of her. Is she aware
of the smallest fish swimming,
does she rejoice at their birth
or feel pain when they are hurt?
Is she moved with the flow of her own
deep currents, though her body,
bounded by shores, is still?

When this water breaks, how far
will you go? No fish, you will walk
on solid legs, while I struggle to hold you
and to let you go. Over and over the ocean
breaks, falling to pieces upon the shore,
but each time she is complete again,
and the sand is softened.

Other End of the Journey
for Chico (1992–2009)

He was a good cat.
His favorite place: a warm lap.
Even when I was pregnant, he curled up
in whatever space was left,
his rounded back tangent
to my belly, asleep within seconds,
despite fetal kicks.

After my daughter was born,
my lap was shared space. He sat
still while she prodded
his paws and legs and whiskers
and ears, only flicking
his tail out of reach. Later,
settling for mechanical warmth,
he lay on the computer all day
while I chopped potatoes
or folded diapers
or bathed and dressed
the little one. But if I sat near enough,
he would gather the strength
to carry his gaunt frame to me.

When my daughter was first born,
she took haphazard breaths, but his last
were steady and smooth, each rising
and falling like an ocean wave,
the fine hairs on his knobby spine
washing over my skin.

Ode to a Midwife

for Amanda

Watching my child peacefully sleeping,
I remember the night I did not sleep.
You gave up sleeping with your husband
in the house with your children. You brought
no instruction, no intrusion, only confidence and calm,
while I dangled between joy and despair. At sunlight's
first gleam through the cracks of the blinds, I gave
one final push. You lifted my daughter and passed her to me.
In those next hours, you lifted me into the bathtub
and out again, tucked me into bed and kissed my forehead. Only then
did you slip out to go. That morning, looking into
my baby's face and seeing the pride in my husband's eyes,
awe gave way to gratitude. I fell asleep with a prayer
that all life could begin with such tireless care.

Birthing

Here is night the way our ancestors knew it,
no clock glowing each excruciating minute.

Here is the midwife saying *intensity*.
Here is the meaning of *strength*.

Here is someone to hold me when I need.
Here is *despair, trust, thirst,* and *joy.*

Here is the morning light forcing its way
through our closed blinds.

Here is your body entering the world,
your head covered with thick hair,

on your face, my own full lips
and my love's long eyelashes.

Here is the air, filling your new lungs.
Here are your bright eyes, open.

Here are your tiny feet, pushing
into my belly from the outside now.

Here is my breast;
here, your small mouth.

Here are the people who treasure you the most.
Here is our room, our humble space in the cosmos.

Here is the sky, under which night always
returns to day, and the earth always holds us.

Nursing

You were born with instincts intact;
I had to learn to hold you and relax,
forget my agendas and attend
ten times a day. You throw
one arm across my body,
fingers kneading my breast. Your eyes,
always so wide, begin to drift.
You float upon the milky ocean, source
of divine nectar and the dark-haired
goddess of prosperity, dressed in gold and red.
Home of the sustainer of the universe,
reclined on his serpent bed,
the lord of time in all its guises:
what we once were, who we might become,
and where we are seated now. You sink into sleep
in my arms. I drink from a glass of water.
Around us, a book, a lamp, a bed, and a clock —
the ordinary shapes of wondrous days.

Bathing

Birds splash
in backyard baths,
otters roll in the sea,
and elephants covered
in grassland dust
pour water overhead
to reveal their stately gray.

In the pool beneath
a waterfall, we
dangle hike-weary feet
and wash the sweat
from our foreheads — part
necessity, part delight.
Back at home, soap and shampoo,
we rid ourselves again of what
we keep getting into.

When you were born
we savoured you
just as you were for seven days
before I poured
warm water over your head. Your hair
shone, a startling
blackness. And then —
a smile
when I had expected a cry.

Imitating

You crane your head back,
lower lip pushed out, tiny fists
raised in salute. We do the same
as we watch you sleep; we can't help
but copy your quirks.

Soon, we'll hold your hands
as you learn to walk
and hold the seat
as you pedal a bike.
We'll teach you letters
and numbers; you'll show us
how to dance and sing.
You'll ride the school bus
without us and fly
to university in a city
we've never seen. You'll study
subjects we could never know,
the way so much of the stuff
of our daily lives
never existed for our parents.

But let's start small.
First, awaken and study
us, eager-eyed daughter,
mimic our open mouths
and raised eyebrows.

Five Months

Practicing delicacy,
your newly opened fingers
twist a strand of my hair.

Window

Late at night, there is the crying.
Crying, crying, crying, crying, and we've done everything
we can think of to comfort her. Nursing
but she pushes me away, walking
outside which quiets her
but doesn't put her to sleep,
and as soon as we're back in the house
it's the crying again.

We walk and hold,
cooing in gentle tones how we don't
understand how we can adore
so intensely. Our pacing
takes us to the window. Looking out,
we describe for our daughter
the lights and trees, stars and
planets we see. She calms, looks out,
looks and looks and looks, rests
her head against my chest and closes her eyes.

Awakening

A giant bug, with bent legs and wings,
grows bigger and bigger on my milk
till it bursts. A red snake, hooded
and fanged, bites at my breast.

*

Bugs repulse my mother, who
smothers them with wet rags.
She will not walk on Rattlesnake Boulevard.
I burst out of childhood
never learning to hold my tongue.

*

From my wounds, blood and water.
From the bug's broken shell, milk
and honey, fragrant and thick.
Inside, a human child
rests her head on my chest,
one arm across my belly,
a bare foot on my thigh. I sing lullabies
and fangs turn into fingers, five
on each hand, clasping
and unclasping, hungry for more.

Naming

At first, you called all of your toy
animals *cat, dog, bunny,* and *lamb.*

Later, they were named after animals in books:
Louise the mouse, and Fred the dog.

Later still, the rhino and the duck and the
others we didn't have stories about,

you named after other characters,
Ollie and Alice, Tony and Jane —

all the names you knew came
from stories we'd read, together.

We chose your name from stories, too —
from myths of gods and goddesses.

Every time we call you, even in
frustration, we invoke immortals.

Sudden Spring

The only things hatching are potholes.
I've always wanted to live near water.

A minefield of thawing shit-bombs in the park.
Ducks swim in circles and quack as I pass.

A bubble somewhere's burst. Bluebirds ask,
Is this where? Is this where, do you know?

The closet is overflowing, every possible
jacket handy. There's no such thing as too early to a party.

Ice finds yet another disguise.
The grass blinks, stunned in the sun.

Raising Daughters

We collect pinecones, point fingers at squirrels,
and jump over a tiny stream
formed by the season's melting snow.
I walk ahead, then turn back with open arms.

The trail is slick with patches of ice. The maple trees,
still bare. I don't remember whether my mother
took me for walks or held my hand.

I see now it must have been so. How sure
I once was of my footing, running
into my mother's arms, ready for her
to hold me close and lift me to the sky.

How to Make Tea

Measure out milk and water,
equal parts. One tea bag
per cup. Cardamom
if desired, sugar to taste.
Cool by pouring from one
cup to another, repeatedly,
each time moving your
hands farther apart.

How to Bless a New Home

Turn your head
when the milk boils. Let it
bubble over. Laugh and make tea
with what is left: it will bring
fortune far greater
than the cost
of the milk you have spilled.

Gods of My Youth

Today I have four arms
and weapons in each hand.
— Jane Munro

The gods of my youth
had many arms and faces,
heads of elephants
and lions, skin blue
or black as the midnight sky.
Some wore flower garlands
and jeweled crowns;
others, necklaces of skulls
or snakes. They rode tigers,
rats, eagles, and peacocks,
and wielded tridents, spears,
and lightning bolts. The hundred
and eight teeth of the discus
would cleanly sever a demon's
head, then return to its bearer
by the next frame of my
Amar Chitra Katha comic.
How could I not have grown up
believing I could do anything?

Recording

We took pictures, in those days,
of your fingernails, eyelashes,
wrinkled feet, and every position
of your hands. We were tipsy with bliss.
Night and day we pictured you.

Spring turned to summer, then to fall.
You learned to sit and crawl, and as
our lives regained rhythm we needed
fewer photos. That's when I started writing:

the story of your birth, your features,
your sleep noises and baby babbling.
How wide you could spread your toes.
Your turtle-faced sleepy stretch.
Pages fill with every fleeting moment,
captured in the black ink of my pen.

Changing Light

Every Morning, Before My Family Wakes, I Invoke Ganesha, God of Beginnings and Lord of Letters

What is description, after all,
but encoded desire?
— Mark Doty

I.

He took a long breath before he began.
Hair tied at the nape of his neck,
skin glowing from his river bath,
he opened his eyes from meditation, took a long breath
and began to speak. In his breath the words were born;
inspiration made meaning from air.

The verses were perfect in diction and meter.
They told a story of kings and fishermen, a saga
of servants and sages. A tale of gods and warriors,
gambling and revenge; duty, disguises, exile,
and snakes. The account begins on a riverbank
and ends with a dog on a mountaintop.

They sat on mats of woven grass beneath
silent banyan leaves. The words left Vyasa's mouth
and began the return into breath.
His tusk dipped in ink, Ganesha made meaning
from black marks on a page. This is how the first poem,
one hundred thousand verses, was written.

II.

We made a baby as I make a poem,
from rapture to the hard work of it.

We watch her grow, take in the world
and learn to take her place in it.
With a rounded mouth she tries out sounds.
With a single finger she draws
the circle of the sun
and opens her hand to show its rays.
Then — words!

Soon she prefers books
over all other toys. If she tramples one
with toddler legs, my daughter kneels
to touch the book then touch her eyes,

a sign of respect
I learned from my parents,
reserved for only books
and gods.

III.

Pen poised between
forefinger and thumb,
middle finger for guidance,
my hand glides left to right,
and my muscles twitch
just so, moving the nib up
and down, over and
around, practiced
movements so quick and subtle
my mind need not linger
on how to command
my nerves and muscles
to make them. Between my brain
and hands, such power lies
to create one mind
of yours and mine.

IV.

My daughter grips her pencil,
awkward as she struggles
to trace the alphabet
I have made. Her lines curve
where they should be straight;
her efforts are clumsy and large.
She tires but starts again,
determined to become
a person of letters.

V.

In my memory we're on the floor, though I know
my father would have insisted we sit at the table.

He watches me copy rows he's written in Malayalam
and teaches me to navigate each letter's tangled lines.
Each curvaceous character forms its own galaxy:

ജ fresh jasmine for my hair, bought on the roadside
before sunrise; ആ the elephant reaches out his trunk
for ripe bananas. My father ഊ greets his brother
after so many years; ഇ a banana leaf for a plate.

*

In India, I walk barefoot with belled anklets ഋ.
My American face മ is out of place; ഷ my shyness, impolite.

At the ashram, a group of children send over a spy,
a boy about five, to see what language I'm writing.
I tilt my notebook toward him, flattered
that they think I can write so easily in Malayalam.
I wonder if he can read English at all,
never mind my cursive scrawl.

*

In grade six, I won a prize for penmanship.
My writing was meticulous, yet
my parents scolded me for taking too long.
I'd practiced the even spacing, right-hand slant,
and carefully connected letters;
years later, I had to learn to scribble.
Even the grammar I mastered young
is hard to disregard. My poetry emerges
in full sentences and paragraphs.

VI.

Inspiration comes
at unexpected times,
even in the evening

in the few minutes
it takes for the cold
pillow to warm.

An image, a line,
a single word
sends out sparks

that light the warehouse
of my gathered
experience. From there,

it's the writing —
it's the writing that makes
things knowable,

that encodes my desire
to live fully
in a small

corner of this vast,
astonishing
world.

Such shine in her eyes
when she learns
a new word.

In the moment
of insight
an object, a single bit

in the sensory
fireworks
of childhood,

becomes a thing
with a name — a name!
Neurons weave

the universe
together with itself,
different in her world

than anyone else's,
and only words
strong enough

to show to all
this tapestry, these colours
only she can see.

VII.

Growing, bearing, mothering . . .
and at last letting go of an infant . . . rapturously
sucks up whole chunks of life.
— Louise Erdrich

Every morning, I put pen to paper until I hear
her clear voice when she awakens.

Yes. *Rapturously* is the right word.
Also *whole chunks of life.*

I close my journal
and turn to embrace my day.

Running Blind

for Peter

On the night we met, you told me to put
my hand inside your elbow, and we set off
down the sidewalk, my senses heightened
for obstacles everywhere: the curb to the right,
the signs and telephone poles to the left,
and coming directly towards us, pedestrians
unaware that you wouldn't shift your course.
Even though the light was green I sensed
your pause as we began to cross the street.

I told you, as we ran, the positions
of people and cars and potholes and puddles.
I told you how the moon was full and about
the rabbit who crossed our path. I tried to tell you
everything that delighted me, like how bright
the sky was that late in the evening, and you agreed
it was a beautiful night, though for you
it was as dark as always. I was suddenly
aware of the poorness of my words
as I tried to describe the blueness of the sky
at that hour, and the way the few beacons
flickered, stars I could barely see.

Giving In

The city now is pinpoints of light,
orange on black, my lamp one piercing blaze.

My husband sleeps; my daughter, too.
Months ago, we moved my desk to the bedroom
so I could nurse our newborn
between poems.

Now her sleepy tosses
and the waves of his breath
creep into my work.

*

Light was the first word she spoke.
Thirty years ago, my first was *light* as well.

When we moved to this apartment
and all the lights were new,
she clapped and laughed as we flipped the switches
over and over
for her.

And every morning we show reverence for the sun;
we eat breakfast turned away, facing our shadows on the wall.

*

I look over from my desk and see
two restless gems in a dark cave.

I abandon my papers, giving in
to her soft dimples, her kicking legs,
and the lustre of her eyes.

*

It's begun. Red rises from the horizon.
The zenith lightens to a bottomless blue,
the hue of a dark and handsome
Hindu god.

The morning star brightens,
then fades. The trees and river appear,
then birds and signs of human society. I bow my head

and turn off my useless lamp.

Learning French

Stepping off the bus
in Chinatown, my ears fill
with syllables I can't decipher:
people choosing pears,
stacking tiles, and
shaking out umbrellas,
all in clear consonants
with open mouths
as if the air
itself were music.

Amidst this melody
I enter my classroom
of breathy vowels,
grunts, and exhalations.
I mould my mouth in new,
curious ways. I collect
French words like a child's
treasures: little rocks in my pockets.

Waiting outside
for the homeward bus,
I whisper to myself: *oiseaux*,
l'arc en ciel. The small boys beside me
point and shout — *căi hóng!*

Learning Malayalam

I teach my daughter a few words
in my mother's mother tongue,
and now she calls me *Amma,*
her father *Achhan,* and I realize
the most harmonious sound I've heard
is a child's Malayalam. Now,

set this poem aside, take a plane to Kerala,
and find a toddler with mischievous eyes.
Close your own and listen
to his luminous, everyday voice:
the tender vowels and intricate
consonants in minute variation,
each sound borne of a particular
point of the palate, the final
breath of every word rising
from the tip of the tongue into song.

Learning Signs

Her signs grew from imitation,
and then the thrill of being understood.
She formed signs with pudgy hands
before she learned to hold a spoon.
She points out dogs and bikes
on our morning walks
with a pat of her thigh
and a pedaling of fists;
at night, she rubs pointer fingers
together towards stars in the sky.
Her words came quickly, but still we sign:
through windows, behind others' backs,
sometimes when there is no reason
not to talk. We face each other
to speak with the whole of our selves,
our meaning plain to see.

Toddlerhood

For washing hands or stepping up
into the car, there's a song
or a phrase that must be repeated
exactly as she's decreed.
When we leave each other, it isn't
a hug but a series of orchestrated
gestures: a head bonk, a nose kiss,
an elbow kiss, a fist bump,
and an ASL *I love you* wave at the end.
Each bit requires a call
and response, where she says
pip and I say *pip-boom*, but that's
just when we're touching noses, see?
We play our parts to perfection, and in turn
these motions make us laugh,
so we're always laughing
whenever we say goodbye.

Lining Up

After we met, I noticed that sometimes
you'd hold your fingers at weird angles
in front of your face. Like,
thumb against your nose, index finger straight up,
middle finger out at about forty-five.

When I asked, you explained that you were lining up
your fingers with the edge of a bookcase,
or the blades of a ceiling fan, or the slats
of the loft you'd built for my dorm room
in the wood shop the previous summer.

I wondered how long we'd have to be together
before your oddities became endearing.
Ten years into our marriage, I happened upon
our daughter lying in bed with her knees crossed
in front of her. She held her right hand close to her face,
squinting as she arranged her fingers. I wanted
to find you just then and say, *this, a decade, this long.*

Blasting Off

At bedtime, all in our pajamas,
we rocketship
and eat pancakes on the moon
or strawberries on Neptune,
meeting friends on asteroids
along the way. We always fly back
to Earth for sleep on our own cozy pillows.
Other nights, it's islands — we paddle or swim
to Madagascar or PEI or Manhattan.
We hike volcanoes, visit museums,
or erect castles out of sand. We don't return home
but sleep at the water's edge,
under a blanket of stars.

Observing the Moon

I.

Sometimes, instead of reading in the evenings,
I take out my binoculars and look up
at the moon. Two weeks ago,
it was round and bright, every tone of light,
a pockmarked face, an ancient lace.

How different from the view
with my naked eyes: a hazy ball of dust,
glimmer of myopic mirage. I imagine
astronomers long ago, spending their nights
gazing at the sky. How can one learn so much
by only looking? The motion of stars
and retrograde planets, when to plant and harvest crops,
the length of the year, the size of our earth,
the orbit and rotation of the moon. . . .

II.

My daughter loves to watch the moon.
Evenings, she sits by the window with me,
and during the day knows just where to spot it,
looking up from the swing in the park.
I follow her pointer to a white half-circle —
the moon, *la lune,* ചന്ദ്രൻ, a crescent shape

made with two small fingers held over her eye
then raised toward the sky. She learns everything
by looking and listening, effortless in her immersion.
Language especially: English, French, Sign,
and Malayalam — not two years old, and

she's at ease when she speaks.
The moon moves, imperceptibly,
nearer to the horizon. She runs up and down the hill,
choosing leaves and acorns to keep, nodding her fist
when I ask if she's ready to go.

III.

While I was pregnant, I took Backyard Astronomy
one night a week during a Michigan winter.
Instead of hoping for clear skies,
our instructor devised a different kind
of star-gazing: in this subject based on observation,
our assignment was just to observe.
So, I wrote detailed notes about the tree
outside my bedroom, the carvings in its bark
and the knotted limbs I'd never noticed.
I sketched the clouds shifting overhead.

One cloudless night, on the university roof,
I peered through a telescope bigger than me to study
Saturn and its perfect rings — small enough
to hold in my palm, a child's spinning toy.
I tried to imagine a windy ball of gas,
so huge and so cold; those delicate rings,
boulders of ice and rock. Titan's tiny glow
seemed too aloof, but those massive bodies
clung to each other with a strength I could not fathom.

Back at home, I paid hard attention
to the movements of my child — felt her
turn and twist, kick and then relax.
I tried to put my findings into words
but ended with only jagged lines on a page.

IV.

Tonight, sitting together by the window,
we're looking at a strand of silver hair
hanging from a tree. My daughter knows
our moon takes many forms.
She trusts the things she can see.

When we first moved to this high-rise,
I saw only the spectacular —
the Ottawa River, the Gatineau hills,
nighttime city lights, and autumn leaves.
But more and more I'm seeing smaller things,
like the foot path worn into the grass
from the dead end of Latchford
to Island Park Drive.

Looking up, I used to see only the moon.
But now I make out a multitude of stars.
The gazelle leaps across the bear's feet;
Orion and his dogs prepare. Auriga drives,
the twins contrive, and Mizar carries Alcor
from her Pleiades sisters, who
wash and dry and plait their midnight hair.

Becoming Canadian

Where will I find
a place I can live and be happy?
— David O'Meara

Finally, I understand:
swearing an oath to the Queen
does not mean promising allegiance
to a person I've never met.
It means the country I have chosen
is personified, the way
the wind and sun quarrel
in Aesop's fable, the way death
drives a carriage in Dickinson's poem.

The judge speaks of our rights
and responsibilities as citizens:
"No one here is above anyone else."
He speaks of religious freedom
and marriage equality; he acknowledges, with a smile,
the baby crying at the back of the room.
Beside me, my daughter munches an apple;
my husband dabs his eyes.
We repeat the oath, in French,
and then in English.

The country I call home
wears tiaras, rides horses, and keeps
a diary. How can I explain
my ease in this place that
gives itself so easily to metaphor?
I shake hands with the judge
and receive the paper that affirms
I am Canadian. My daughter looks up
and hands me her apple core; I bend
down to kiss her Canadian cheek.

Summer's End

I leave all the windows open. Why
go anywhere? I sit outside and breathe.

A yellow edge appears on emerald leaves.
Braids of garlic at the market. Cheeky squirrels.

The air smells of far-off fire. We lie naked
beneath the ceiling fan. We don't make up our minds.

The season lingers between toes. Sand
on our pillows, in every corner of the house.

My daughter remarks, how sad it would be
to live in a world that never, ever changes.

Notes

Out of the Blue
Italicized lines are a mnemonic for the colour-coded forecasts of the weather beacon atop the Berkeley Building (also called the Old John Hancock Tower) in Boston. During baseball season, flashing red lights signal that the Red Sox game is cancelled due to weather.

Mothering
The epigraph by Heather McHugh is from the preface to *Hinge & Sign: Poems 1968–1993* (Wesleyan University Press, 1994).

Gods of My Youth
The epigraph by Jane Munro is from the poem "Old Man Vacanas" (*Blue Sonoma,* Brick Books, 2014).

Every Morning, Before My Family Wakes, I Invoke Ganesha, God of Beginnings and Lord of Letters
The epigraph by Mark Doty is from the poem "Description" (*Fire to Fire: New and Selected Poems,* HarperCollins, 2008).

The epigraph by Louise Erdrich is from *The Blue Jay's Dance: A Birth Year* (HarperCollins, 1995).

Becoming Canadian
The epigraph by David O'Meara is from the poem "Walking Around" (*The Vicinity,* Brick Books, 2003).

Acknowledgements

Poems in this book have previously appeared in *The Antigonish Review, Arc Poetry Magazine, Branch, The Birth Project, Descant, FreeFall, The Huron River Review, ottawater, The Prairie Journal, Room,* the Leaf Press Monday's Poem series, and my chapbook, *Some Things With Certainty* (Phafours Press).

An earlier version of *Observing the Moon* was a finalist for the Writers' Federation of New Brunswick's 2013 Alfred G. Bailey Prize.

I am grateful for the support, guidance, and friendship of so many people, far too many to name here. Warmest thanks to you all, especially to the vibrant community of writers in Ottawa.

Thanks to my editor, Harold Rhenisch, for his insight and keen knowledge of craft.

I owe much to Deborah Bayer, who set me on the path toward the writing life.

Gratitude and love to John Madhavan-Reese, first reader of these poems and my partner in so many things, and to our daughters, Anasuya and Shailaja, masters of observation.

Thanks also to the City of Ottawa and the Ontario Arts Council for financial support during the writing of this book.

Sneha Madhavan-Reese was born in Detroit and now lives with her family in Ottawa. She has degrees in Engineering from MIT and the University of Michigan. Her poetry has appeared in literary journals in the U.S. and Canada, including *Arc Poetry Magazine, Descant,* and *The New Quarterly.* Winner of the Diana Brebner Prize, she was also a finalist for the Montreal International Poetry Prize, the Far Horizons Award for Poetry, and the Alfred G. Bailey Prize.